A Gap Year

Volunteering

The College Student's Guide

Jason Birkenstock

INTENTION

Printed in the United States of America

First Printing, 2014

ISBN: 978-1-495917-30-1

For all author questions, speaking engagement requests, and bulk purchase pricing please contact Intention Publishing at: intentionpublishers@gmail.com

Editors: Savonna Greer, Mark Balog, and Aly Loriezo

This book is dedicated to my parents, Paul and Sandra Birkenstock. Without your continual support and guidance, my gap year volunteering and in turn this book would never have been possible.

Contents

Contents

Contents

Contents

Contents

Contents

Foreword

My name is Jason Birkenstock and I am writing this book because I want to share my volunteer experience and in the process hopefully allow others to benefit from the lessons I have learned. I am currently serving as a volunteer English teacher in Santo Domingo, Ecuador. So far, it has been one of the best decisions of my life. I have been challenged in many ways, met some of the most incredible people, and discovered just how gratifying teaching can be.

Something that readers should know about me is that I am not a formally trained teacher nor do I aspire to be one. Above all else, I am just a recent college graduate who chose to take a gap year and spend it teaching English and traveling South America. I firmly believe that regardless of your area of study, economic standing, or future plans, if you have a desire to take a year out volunteering and experiencing life, you should...and you can.

In this book, you will find a wide variety of information, including how to decide, prepare, pack, and survive. It is intended for 18-24 year olds in the United States who are considering taking a gap year to volunteer. While much of the information is based upon my personal experience as a volunteer in Ecuador, nearly all of the information remains a valuable resource for volunteers regardless of their intended destination. I have organized this book as a reference guide, ready to be consulted at any point during the volunteer process. I sincerely hope that you find it informative, entertaining, and above all else useful!

The Decision

This is probably the most crucial step in the entire process. You have to decide. That's it. Take the leap and just decide to take a year or two out of your life and have an adventure while giving back to society. I know it's scary and if you are anything like me (a hardcore, type A choleric) it is a concept that is completely alien to you. You probably want to know where exactly you will be, what you will and won't have access to, and what your job description will entail...I am telling you right now, that won't happen. An inherent part of this experience is adventure, a fact that will make it an incredibly exhilarating and rewarding experience.

However, please don't mistake my message. I am not saying to just jump blindly into this, but rather that the most important part of the decision is that you commit to spending a year volunteering for your own carefully planned out, personal reasons. This way, if circumstances are not what you expect, your core decision to volunteer will not be affected. It is the only way to fully embrace the experience and remain content throughout it.

My Decision

It was 2012 and I was fast approaching graduation from Walla Walla University. I was an extremely involved student—taking full loads, working for the student association, and assisting a local defense attorney. As you might guess, I had aspirations to go to law school (I still do!). I had taken the LSAT (Law School Admission Test) the summer before with little preparation and had unsurprisingly received a mediocre score...a phenomenon I was not used to. Having such a score left me considering all of my options. I was constantly thinking, "Should I just nix the whole law school idea and go into business? Should I retake the LSAT? Should I go to business school for my MBA? Or, the more fun but seemingly least responsible option, should I just say peace out everyone and head overseas to spend a year volunteering and traveling with the money I don't have." I played around with all of these options. I went to a few interviews, applied to a few mediocre law schools with my mediocre LSAT score,

13

researched some volunteer organizations, and bought a GMAT prep book. My heart wasn't fully in any of these endeavors and my days were already filled with my collegiate responsibilities.

It was in the midst of this that I received a surprisingly generous full ride scholarship offer to a rather low-end law school. All of a sudden, I had four weeks to make a decision. This was an agonizing time for me. I knew that the law school wasn't great, but you really can't beat free. However, I was not ready to commit to this law school and rule out all of the other options I was considering. With family pressure, economic pressure, and mixed responses from friends, I was in desperate need of a bit of soul searching for a definitive answer.

I spent time journaling, praying, talking, emailing, and everything in between. However, in the end, my final decision came after one of my oldest and best friends asked me a very simple question.

"In 10 years, when you look back, what will you regret the most? That you didn't go straight to graduate school after college or that you didn't take year out and volunteer?"

Although a rather simple question, it was just what I needed. After being bogged down in the many details surrounding my options, I needed a reminder to take a step back and look at the core of the decision. Once I did this, it was crystal clear—I would most definitely, without a doubt, regret not taking a year out to volunteer. I can clearly remember thinking, "When else will I the time and freedom to just ditch everything for a year and volunteer in another country? Possibly never. Everything else can easily wait one year." Just like that, I had reached a decision.

On the following page is a decision guide that will hopefully help you do the same.

Decision Guide

Option	#1 _____	#2 _____	#3 _____
Benefits	1. 2. 3. 4. 5.	1. 2. 3. 4. 5.	1. 2. 3. 4. 5.
Drawbacks	1. 2. 3. 4. 5.	1. 2. 3. 4. 5.	1. 2. 3. 4. 5.
Can it be done 5 years from now?			
Does my family support it?			
Do I want to do it?			
Final Decision			

Commit

Hopefully, after utilizing the decision guide, the best alternative is clear. There's nothing like a good grid with a pro/con list to make you face facts. However, sometimes it takes a few permanent actions to fully commit to this decision. It was only after I had done this that I felt at peace with my decision. Now I am not talking about just calling Mom and Dad and saying that today you have decided to become a volunteer, because for all they know tomorrow you will decide to be a doctor, and the day after an astronaut. No, the commitment I am talking about is much more serious than a simple phone call home.

I am talking about not applying for any graduate programs and not interviewing for internships or potential postgraduate jobs that will conflict with your gap year. I am talking about declining opportunities to be involved in campus clubs and groups for the following year. The best way to make you stay true to a decision is to leave yourself with just that one option. When you have only one option, you make it work; it's human nature! —Use it to your advantage!

The Organization

Now that you have committed to spending your next year as a volunteer, it's time to start looking at how to go about doing it. Perhaps the first and most important step you need to take is deciding which organization (or lack thereof) that you are going to utilize. There are many great organizations that facilitate volunteer efforts throughout the world. You have the Peace Corps, arguably the most renowned volunteer organization, various church organizations, private companies that provide placements for a fee, etc. Naturally, these various entities range in both prestige and professionalism. All of them will get you overseas and volunteering. However, before you decide, there are a few things that you will want to take into consideration such as length of service, reputation of the organization, and level of guidance provided.

Note: In Appendix A there is a list of helpful websites that can direct you to various organizations.

Time

Many different organizations have specific time commitments that they require of their volunteers. In general, the more time and resources an organization is willing to invest, the longer they expect their volunteers to serve. A prime example of this is the Peace Corps.

When I was considering what organization to volunteer through, I first looked at the Peace Corps. I found that they prepare you for your time overseas with language and culture education, have standing relationships with the graduate admissions programs of many of America's finest universities, and assume some liability for you while you are overseas. However, with this level of surety, they fairly ask for 18 months of service. Unfortunately, this simply did not fit into my graduate school plans or my student loan repayment plans, so they were not the organization I ended up using.

At the other end of the spectrum are shorter 3 to 5 week volunteer trips that focus on short-term goals or projects. While these are great for those with limited time, they generally do not meet the criteria of a full gap year volunteering, so I am not going to spend any additional time on them.

The moral of this short section is that you must check and see what the required length of volunteer time is. No matter how great the organization, if you can't make the time frame work, it just wasn't meant to be.

Reputation

As I mentioned earlier, some volunteer organizations have phenomenal reputations capable of aiding you in graduate school applications and future employment searches. However, for me at least, I was more concerned with an organization's reputation in regards to how well they took care of their volunteers and what their motivation was for sending out volunteers. While researching online I came across some organizations that charged obscene prices that made me wonder just how altruistic they really were. Although I do not have any personal experience with shoddy volunteer organizations, I caution you to take your time and look at online blogs and news articles regarding each one. Generally if there is a problem with an organization, it will pop up pretty quickly.

Level of Guidance

This is a matter of personal preference. If you are a more nervous person by nature, it may be a good idea to look for an organization that provides their volunteers with lots of guidance in regards to visas, travel arrangements, and teaching/cultural training. Naturally, there will always be an element of the unknown, but that does not mean that extra preparation and guidance is a bad idea. You want to push your limits, but not go so far as to find yourself in a situation that you are simply not equipped to handle.

Most organizations do provide some basic instruction and education. However, as I said earlier, the smaller the organization/volunteer time the less guidance and personal attention you can expect. If you are adventurous by nature and don't feel as though you need much additional guidance then feel free to take a chance on the obscure organization that may be lacking in that area. The most important thing is to know yourself and how much surety you require.

My Decision

After much research and online fact checking, I discovered that the absolute best organization for me ended up being the one at my school, Walla Walla University. They coordinate over 80 student volunteers each year around the world. Additionally, they are associated with a worldwide church (Seventh-day Adventist) that allows them to provide the guidance and resources of a larger organization. In the end, it was just so convenient—I was able to talk with past volunteers who had returned from their gap year, I knew students who worked in the volunteer office, and they had specific job descriptions from around the world that were posted by the various institutions in need of a volunteer. If your school has a volunteer or study abroad office, they will most likely be the best, most accessible resource for your volunteering plans. Utilize them as much as possible!

The Place

Now this is probably what you have been visualizing the most when considering volunteering. You picture yourself helping in a Nigerian orphanage or perhaps teaching English in South Korea. Maybe it is educating elementary school kids in the islands of Micronesia or perhaps helping improve the infrastructure of an Amazonian tribe. There are many exotic places that encompass both terrific need and spectacular surroundings. Some might say that this shouldn't matter, that serving should be the only thing that's on your mind, but I just don't think that's realistic. I mean you are giving up a year of your life to volunteer, why not have a bit of fun thinking and planning what exotic places you can see along the way? I say you deserve it!

Organizational Limitations

Now, there are a couple of important things to consider when choosing the region where you will be volunteering. The first should be pretty obvious and that is the limitations of the organization you have chosen to volunteer through. Some organizations focus on primarily one area of the world or one specific type of volunteer work (medical, educational, engineering, etc.). Naturally, you can only perform a specific type of volunteer service in a city or country where your organization is active.

Language

The second thing you should consider is language. Do you know a second language that you would like to strengthen? Or is there perhaps a language that you have always wanted to learn or that you see as potentially useful in your future career. Again, I say work this experience in every way possible. You are volunteering for a year; why not kill two birds with one stone?

You should be aware though, that if you chose to go to a region where you are unfamiliar with the language, it will be challenging. You will have to put time into learning the language, at least until you get to a point where you can get around reasonably well. At the beginning it can be somewhat lonely spending your days surrounded by people speaking a foreign language, trying to get to know them through hand gestures and limited phrases. It will be frustrating and at times overwhelming. However, the good news is, it's temporary. Being completely immersed in a language increases your ability to pick up the language tenfold. Also, I have found that spending an hour a day studying sentence structure and verb conjugations speeds up the process even more. Although initially difficult, the language can be one of the most rewarding aspects of your experience.

Surrounding Regions

The third thing to consider is the surrounding regions and locations. Is there a part of the world you have always wanted to explore? There may never again be a time when you will have a place to call home for an extended period of time overseas. Remember, there will be holidays, breaks, and impromptu trips with new friends that will open up an entirely new part of the world. The beauty of this is that all of these trips will be relatively inexpensive because they don't include a pricey international flight like they would if you were visiting from back in America. Whether your interests lie in somewhere as remote as Antarctica, or as urban as Hong Kong or Europe, don't be afraid or ashamed to look for volunteer opportunities there. Again, you are

VOLUNTEERING for a year. Don't be ashamed to work your interests into your planning. Do it right and you can spend a year doing some good and crossing a few things off your bucket list!

Type of Work

The fourth thing you should take into consideration is the type of work you want to do. I have placed this after organizational limitations, language, and surrounding regions because more often than not the work you thought you would be doing is not the majority of what you end up doing or at the very least, it is not what you expected it to be like. Wherever you are volunteering, you will most likely discover that there is a huge amount of need that creates a broad variety of positions that you can easily jump into. Granted, if you absolutely hate the idea of teaching or working in a jungle you probably shouldn't pursue positions that stress those things because at the very least, it will still be a small part of your experience. However, I urge you not to rule things out too easily. In my experience, it is those things that you thought you would never enjoy doing that make for the best experiences.

For example, I definitely had just about no teaching experience before coming to Ecuador and I can't say that I was particularly fond of kids in general. But now, 5 months in, I absolutely love teaching my high school English classes. They are challenging, hilarious, and a daily reminder of how much fun kids are, especially in high school. I even miss my students a tiny bit while traveling over breaks.

Flexibility

The fifth and final thing you should remember when choosing a place to volunteer is that you must, absolutely must, be flexible. Have a first, second, and third choice of where you want to volunteer. This is where you have to be careful not to go too far on the "I'm volunteering and deserve it" spectrum; you are going to volunteer and that should ultimately be your number one purpose...with traveling and experiencing another culture as a close second. Remember, volunteer positions are finicky by nature. They are advertised and handled by organizations filled with overworked and under assisted individuals...hence the existence of a volunteer position at their organization. It is not uncommon for positions to remain advertised or posted even after they have been filled, so do not get discouraged if you hit a few brick walls. The key is to remember to be flexible and be willing to consider countries or regions that you had not previously thought of.

As a perfect example, I originally had hopes of going to Spain for my volunteer year, but by the end of the process I found myself on a plane to Ecuador—two countries that are worlds apart. While initially disappointed, I hopped online and quickly discovered the multitude of pristine vistas and unique cities and experiences that South America holds. And now, after about 5 months here and quite a bit of travel, I have no regrets! South America is absolutely beautiful and is filled with some of the friendliest people I have ever met.

Unexpected Road Blocks

So now you have committed to your year of volunteering and have even secured a specific volunteer position in a foreign country. Everything seems to be coming together nicely, but then all of a sudden you hit a roadblock. Your student loans may not be able to be deferred or you hear about some awful experience another volunteer had in the past. It's times like these that you feel tempted to go into back up plan mode and start trying to reverse some of those permanent steps you took—sending in last minute grad school applications or putting out feelers for potential leadership roles around campus for next year—it's just in case, right? Wrong! Don't do it! Don't freak out! Just remember that you committed to this. You CAN and you WILL make it work. Below are a few helpful tips to overcome various obstacles that you might encounter, some of which I faced and others that I was lucky enough to avoid.

Student Loans

If you are anything like me, you have incurred some student loan debt. While you may not have had to think about this much while in school, you will quickly find out that within a few months of no longer having full time student status, those loan payments will start rolling in. The last thing you want is to be in a foreign country, trying to talk with a loan company over a shaky connection, with very little to say except for, "Sorry, I wanted to take a break and do some good. I know I owe you money, but I definitely can't get it to you right now...I'm in Timbuktu!"

The good news is that if you plan correctly, you won't have to deal with this. Months before I left, I checked with my student loan companies about deferring my loan payments. To my surprise, I found that it is actually a pretty simple process. I guess it's not that uncommon for people to try and defer their loans...surprise, surprise. So, all that you, the future volunteer, have to do is contact your respective loan company (Sallie Mae, Nelnet, etc.) and see what their policy is on deferments. Often times you can do this on their website. Because you are a volunteer that means you will have $0 income, which qualifies you for an Economic Hardship Deferment for a limited amount of time, generally about six months, which will be more than enough time for you to get back to school, and reclaim that full time student status. Remember, loans only become due 6 months after you stop school, and then if you get a 6 month deferment, that means that you will have a 12 month window for volunteering.

What happens if your loan company doesn't have the Economic Hardship Deferment? No problem. Nearly all of the major private student loan companies allow for a loan to be deferred for an extended period of time (about 27 months in total) over the life of the loan for any reason. This means you can just defer them for 6 months, as long as you realize that in the future you now only have 21 months of deferment at your disposal if you have a time of unemployment or if any other unsavory circumstances arise.

Just remember that when it comes to student loans you can and will get it deferred. I mean, you are one of how many tens of thousands of students who have student loan debt. Your request is not an unusual one and it is motivated by a selfless desire to give back to society. Use that and make it happen!

Note: The above deferment also applies to parent plus loans and other student loans your parents may have taken out on your behalf.

31

Visas

Visas are a pain in the butt, plain and simple. The first thing you should know is that you will have to go to the consulate of the country where you are planning on volunteering in order to obtain a visa. This is required for you to legally reside in just about any foreign country for more than a few months. Depending on how obscure the country is, you may have to travel to New York, Washington DC, or San Francisco, which can be expensive. However, most countries have consulates on both the west and east coasts.

The other thing that makes visas annoying are that often times the requirements change from consulate to consulate or they differ from what the consulate website says. The best thing to do is go online and check the consulate website and find out what all they require. Once you've done this, call the consulate and ask them to tell you what the requirements are. This way you cover all your bases. It is best to start this process 4 to 6 months before you depart. Often times countries will require certain vaccinations, which will entail several trips to your local physician for different phases of the vaccination. Also, they will require a sizeable fee to be paid for processing (I have no idea why), bank account information, a valid passport (if you don't have one, this can be a 2 month process in itself), separate passport photos, and additional paperwork from the organization you will be volunteering at.

This means that you will have to email that organization multiple times and make sure that they send you all of the documents the consulate requires. It can be a time consuming, painfully slow process. That is why it is KEY that you give yourself plenty of time.

When you finally do go and visit the consulate, bring every piece of information and paperwork that you have. It's much easier for them to give you back extra papers that they don't need than it is for you to make a second trip because you forgot some obscure copy of the country's constitution or some other ridiculous requirement.

Grad School Applications

Again, if you are anything like me, you have future educational plans after your year of volunteering. This means that you will need to plan on studying and taking any required tests (GMAT, LSAT, MCAT, SAT, etc.) prior to your departure. You will also need to prepare any application essays, personal statements, resumes, and in person interviews before you leave. I personally have gone through this process and found that most institutions are more than happy to work with you and your volunteer constraints. Whether this means they interview you via Skype or provide you with an application before they load them up to their website, most graduate schools or colleges are more than happy to do it. Both undergraduate and graduate schools are in the business of getting quality people to come to their institutions and generally people who take a year out to give back and increase their exposure with other cultures are just that—quality people. They will work with you and if they don't, they probably aren't an institution you would want to attend anyways.

The key is advance planning. Make sure you know when applications become available, what test scores they require, and when the applications are due. If you contact them ahead of time with any time constraint concerns they will be much more willing to work with you than if you email them last minute, looking like an unprepared candidate who didn't have the foresight to plan ahead.

Lame People

Some people are just going to rain on your parade. They may say it's irresponsible to stop your education for a year and waste time "messing around" in a foreign country. These people are narrow-minded individuals who most likely just lack the courage to do what you are doing, or if they are older, regret that they didn't do it themselves. When you encounter these people, don't even argue. Hear them out, say, "thanks for the input," and then just ignore it. You're not going to change their mind and as long as you have carefully thought out why you are taking your year out, they should have absolutely no bearing on your decision. If you require some reassurance, just bust out that handy decision grid you filled out earlier and read all of those benefits. There's no one like you to reassure yourself.

Vaccinations

Although I mentioned vaccinations earlier, I feel as though they warrant a second mention. I highly suggest that once you know where you will be serving for a year that you contact your primary care physician and inform him or her of your travel plans. Most likely he or she will refer you to an associated travel clinic that specializes in immunizations and has helpful brochures regarding the area of the world where you will be volunteering.

Before you have your appointment with your doctor/travel clinic nurse, spend some time thinking about what nearby regions and/or nearby countries you might travel to. They will ask you this and depending on your answer may recommend some additional immunizations.

Also, they may give you the option to take some immunizations that are not required (i.e. Rabies). My personal philosophy is to plan for the worst and get vaccinated for everything possible.

35

The last place where you want to be is in a foreign hospital with limited resources and medical equipment fighting a random virus that could have easily been prevented with a vaccination that was readily available back in good old America.

So, take a deep breath, roll up those sleeves, and get all the vaccinations you can!

Money

This is a pretty common potential roadblock, but as always you can overcome it. Inform family, friends, your church, past schools, your dentist, the mailman, absolutely EVERYONE of your plans to spend a year volunteering via a fundraising letter and provide a paid for return envelope that they can send a contribution in. If you are going through a nonprofit organization, often times they can provide a tax-deductible receipt for those who contribute to your trip. While this letter and the associated thank you cards may cost a bit to send out, it will most likely prove to be well worth it.

Another option is to be creative in finding ways to generate funds. Often times there are plenty of items (bikes, skis, a seldom-used piano, a junker car, etc.) lying around the house or in the garage that can be put up on Craigslist or eBay. Old clothes can be sold to consignment stores and books to used bookstores.

Yet another option is to make a unique product that you can sell online or in person. I have had friends create and sell t-shirts with designs that reflect their future country, specially labeled bottles of water, baked pies, and much more. Every $1 counts!

Finally, and probably the most obvious, is to look for additional work that will allow you to pay for any costs associated with your trip (plane ticket, visa processing, etc.).

Remember, you have committed to this and it is now your only option. Get intentional and get creative about fundraising!

Airplane Ticket

This is most likely what makes up the largest part of the cost of serving as a volunteer. All you can do is check all of the websites on a daily basis well ahead of time and look for the best price possible. Make sure that you check with the organization where you will be volunteering if there is a specific airport where they would like you to fly into that they can pick you up at.

Note: In Appendix B, I have included a list of the websites that I found had the best prices.

Final Preparation

At this point, you have your visa in hand, a valid passport is sitting on your desk, your ticket has been purchased, and you are realizing that in just a month or two you will be leaving the country for an extended period of time. It is both exciting and nerve-racking. You want to make sure that you don't forget to tie up any loose ends. You worry that you may lose touch with those who are important to you and miss out on major life events of family and friends. All of these concerns are normal and can be put to rest. Below I have included a list of things that you should make sure you have addressed before you leave. Most of them are things that I did prior to my departure and a few are things that I wish I had done. I hope it helps bring you some peace before your departure.

Contact the Place You Will Be Volunteering At

Send them an email and ask them the following questions:

- Is there a dress code I need to plan for?

- Do I need to bring school supplies, teaching materials, or other items essential to performing my volunteer duties?

- What is the name of the person who will be picking me up? How will I find them?

- What is the mailing address where I will be staying?

- What is the weather like?

- Are there any essential items I should be absolutely sure to bring?

Simplify the Life You Are Leaving Behind

Sort through your belongings and make some trips to the Goodwill or list unwanted items on

Craigslist. You will feel so much more at ease when you depart if the life you are leaving behind is in good order and filled with items that you have purposefully chosen. It will also make your return that much more enjoyable.

Buy a Journal

I know, I know, this already sounds so cliché, but hear me out. I never, and I repeat NEVER, have been one for journaling. It always felt unnatural and honestly a waste of time. However, I was wrong—so wrong! Before you leave and while you are away, you will be doing lots of introspection, experiencing a new culture, and making future plans. These thoughts, plans, and experiences are pure gold and are something you will want to look at later, especially before you return. It is a surefire way to guarantee that you will be able to recognize how this experience has changed you and what your mindset was prior to your departure. It is a wonderfully clarifying practice.

Also, perhaps an even more important reason why you should journal is that it will help you avoid forgetting the details surrounding the many amazing experiences you will have. Before I left, the one thing in common that every past volunteer said was that they wished that they had written down more of their experiences or even just the names of the people they met. It is amazing how quickly you forget what happened, where you were, and who you were with. Do yourself a favor and write things down. It will enable lessons and experiences to remain a source of enjoyment for years to come and even allow others an insight into your experience if you decide to share it.

Finally, please note that when I talk about journaling, I don't mean for you to sit down every day and write out every detail of your life. That is so boring. Write when you have something to write about. Some weeks here I have nothing to write about, so I don't. No big deal. However, when those good times and crazy experiences happen, I write them down and so should you!

So, trust me on this, go out and buy a journal. You won't regret it.

Friendships—

Be Intentional

Spend some time thinking about the friendships you have, identifying those that are a positive influence in your life and those that detract from it (Journal it!). When you are overseas, you will have to actively put time and effort into staying in contact with those who are important to you. Those who are not, generally fall by the wayside. It's natural, and probably one of the best ways to sever unhealthy friendships with the least amount of pain or anger. Also, you will quickly realize that those who value your friendship will be those who make an effort to contact you and hear about your adventures, making sure that you are still alive and kicking in whatever random country you find yourself in. It is amazing just how clarifying a year away can be in this regard.

Relationships—

<u>Have a Plan</u>

Honestly, this is a pretty personal decision that you have to make. I cannot say whether you should break up, take a break, stay together, get married beforehand, or anything in between. But what I can tell you is that it is important for both you and your significant other to know exactly where you both are at before leaving. If you decide to stay together, figure out how you will communicate and perhaps even plan a trip for them to come and visit. Know that it can be challenging to maintain a relationship with limited internet capability, different time zones, and completely different environments. It is not impossible though. I have had many good friends not only maintain their relationships, but improve them in the long run during times of only long-distance connectivity. Granted, this has not been my experience, but hey, it might be yours.

I also feel that it is important to remind you that just as with unhealthy friendships, a time away in a different country is a great reason to end an unhealthy relationship with the least amount of collateral damage. If you have concerns about your relationship, remember that this will be a time of great self-discovery and clarity, one that may require you to be unhindered by a relationship filled with past baggage. It really comes down to where you and your significant other are at in the relationship.

So, in conclusion, make sure you have that tough conversation and get on the same page before you step onto that plane.

Family—

Make Them a Priority

You are going to miss a year's worth of birthdays, holiday celebrations, and everyday interactions that may not seem like much now, but can be what you miss the most. While this is somewhat sad, it is a reality and thus something that you should intentionally plan for. This means spending lots of time with brothers, sisters, parents, aunts, uncles, grandparents, and other people in your life who are like family prior to your departure. Remember, while this is an amazing experience for you, often times it can be hard on those who love and support you. Mom's in particular are notorious for supporting you at every turn, but spending the whole drive back from dropping you off at the airport in tears...well mine is at least. Haha!

Additionally, realize that those grandparents, elderly uncles, and aunts that have been a source of inspiration and guidance in your life are in reality human, and it is possible that their health will fail while you are away. God-willing this is not something that you will face, but it is something that you may have to. Make sure that you spend time with them before you leave. The harsh reality is that it may be the last time you see them. This unfortunately goes for anyone in your life. Don't get too concerned or start bawling your eyes out though; most likely everything will be fine and you will see them in a few months. Just be sure to cover all your bases.

Plan out How

You Will Communicate

Decide whether you are going to bring your laptop or if you are going to stick with an iPod or iPhone. My personal suggestion is to bring something small and portable like an iPod that has

Wi-Fi accessibility and a front camera for Skyping purposes. Although if you are teaching, it may well be worth it to bring an inexpensive netbook or low-end laptop. I am currently rocking a 2008 Windows XP netbook and a 2009 iPod and am surviving!

Also, create a Skype account and purchase some credit for any time you need to make an important call to family or friends on their cell phone.

Finally, make sure you tell friends and family how they can reach you and gather any needed information. Something that I should have done, but didn't, was write down everyone's cell phone number and physical address. This makes life so much easier when it comes time to send postcards and get in contact with friends and family in a hurry. It is amazing how seldom we need to actually memorize phone numbers. You quickly realize upon arrival that you only know a few numbers by memory, which means a whole bunch of emails and Facebook messages have to be sent. Save yourself the time and trouble and do this beforehand.

Make Future Plans

Before you leave, I highly suggest making plans for when you return to go on a trip or to meet up with those friends you have identified as important in your life. This will bring lots of peace when you have those moments of worry that you will lose touch with all of those people who are important to you. It will also give you something to look forward to during those times in your volunteer year when you are feeling a bit disconnected or perhaps even homesick.

Back Up Your Computer

If you take a computer, this is an absolute must. Buy an external hard drive or simply back up your computer to a desktop at home. I cannot stress how important this is. All of your photos, music, and every document you have ever created lie in the balance.

I stress this so much because my own computer was stolen during the customs process when I headed out on my volunteer year. The only thing that made it nothing more than an unfortunate occurrence was that I had completely backed it up the night before I left...that and the insurance money the airline paid me. ☺

Scan Travel Documents

This is another one of those must do things. I did it and it has saved me countless times. Take twenty minutes and scan in your passport, driver's license, credit card, visa documents, airline tickets, and absolutely any other document that you deem essential. Once you have done this, email them to yourself and stick it in a special folder within your email. This means that if your bag is stolen, you misplace your passport, lose your credit card, or anything else, it is as simple as going into your email and printing out a copy of it. Trust me; you will be glad you did this.

Alert Bank &

Credit Card Company

Call your bank and credit card company and provide them with the dates that you will be out of the country. If you don't do this, they will see unexpected international charges, assume your identity has been stolen, and freeze all your accounts. The last thing you want is to be stuck in a foreign country without access to your money.

Also, if you don't have a credit card in addition to your debit card, I highly suggest applying for one. They are extremely cheap to use overseas and allow an added level of security because you cannot withdraw money with a credit card. This means that if a pickpocket steals it or worse, they try and force you to withdraw money from your bank, it is impossible to draw out physical cash. Also, it is much easier to reverse fraudulent charges on a credit card than a debit card.

Update Social Network Profiles

Make sure you update your Facebook, LinkedIn, Twitter, Instagram, and whatever other social media you frequent to reflect that you will be out of the country for an extended period of time. This will serve two purposes. First, it will avoid any friends or relations from thinking that you are being rude when you don't answer messages in a timely manner. Second, if you are applying to graduate schools, it will make you look especially put together and prepared because many of those institutions do look at your online presence during the application process.

Cancel or Downgrade Your Cell Phone

Since you won't be in the US for an extended period of time, you might as well save yourself (or your parents) the $50 a month it costs by either cancelling or suspending your contract.

One word of advice though, if you are sending in applications to grad schools, you definitely want an active voicemail stating that you are out of the country and that the best way to contact you is via email. If you completely cancel/suspend your contract there will be no voicemail. However, if you just downgrade it to the lowest, no texting, data free, plan you can still save a solid $30 a month.

If you still receive assistance from your parents and they are generous, they may even be willing to deposit that extra money they are saving into your checking account while you are gone. Never hurts to ask right?

Cancel or Downgrade Your Car Insurance

If you have a car, you should definitely call your insurance company and suspend your coverage. They may still have you pay a nominal monthly fee ($10 or so), but this will save you (or your parents) hundreds of dollars while you are away volunteering.

Remember to check with your parents and see if you can possibly benefit from the savings.

Check Your Medical and Traveler's Insurance

It is always a good idea to make sure that you know exactly what your medical insurance covers out of the country and where exactly is the closest place in that country where you can receive medical treatment.

Also, check any life insurance or homeowner's insurance you or your parents have to see whether or not they will pay if any of your more pricey items are stolen while overseas. In all honesty, if they don't, it's no big deal. You shouldn't be bringing anything with an exorbitant value. The highest valued item will probably be at most a $1,000 camera or laptop.

The Packing List

At this point, you are maybe a week away from leaving. You have addressed and taken care of each of the points covered in the previous section and are now just facing the exciting and annoying task of packing your bags. I have included what I packed, how many bags I took, and the reasoning behind it. Hopefully it helps you. Just remember, less is more. You can always buy more clothes or unforeseen necessities at your volunteer location. It will just take some effort and a willingness to use unfamiliar products.

Note: Take into consideration that this packing list is written from the male perspective. Ladies—adapt as needed.

Carry-on Bag

- Kindle

    o Books are heavy. Why not go digital? You can buy an old Kindle online for $80 and have access to the largest bookstore in the world, 24-7. Worth it!

- IPod

    o Long bus rides, plane trips, and even odd nightly noises are all phenomenal reasons for why you should bring an iPod. It WILL save your sanity on multiple occasions.

- Headphones

    o Bring at least two pairs of headphones. I suggest the iPhone ones that have a speaker built into them. This way you can Skype via your iPod.

- Computer

    o I don't suggest that you bring your expensive MacBook or PC, especially if there is high humidity where you are going. Instead, snag a cheap netbook or tablet for $150. That way if something happens to it, it's okay. Additionally, being able to create exams, keep track of grades, and watch the occasional movie are all great reasons to bring a cheap computer.

- USB Drive

  o I didn't bring this and it has been such a pain. Make sure you pack one with at least 8 GB.

- Camera(s)

  o You will most definitely want to have a camera with you to remember all of the amazing things you see. I have found the Canon Powershot series to be a wonderfully compact, durable option that produces great photos. Also, if you are a photography enthusiast, take the risk and bring your DSLR camera. Yes, it makes you look like a tourist and yes it might even make you a target for pickpockets, but why did you buy it in the first place? To take amazing photos. You will possibly never have another experience so rich with photographable subjects as this one.

- Journal

    - I've talked about this plenty. Just make sure you get it in the bag. I would highly suggest carrying it onto the plane with you. I will explain why later.

- 3x5 cards

    - While this is technically a school supply, you will find them amazingly useful for just about everything (birthday cards, addresses, notes, etc.).

- Travel book

    - Go and buy a guidebook for the country you will be volunteering in. Spend some time perusing it. It will give you great information regarding travel destinations and experiences you should pursue.

- Dictionary/Language Guide

    - Buy a dictionary that includes both English and the native language of the country you will be residing in. Often times there are great compact travelling dictionaries that include the most necessary words/phrases and are not as cumbersome to use. I brought both.

- Cash

  - Pull out a solid $200 (no bills higher than $20) before you leave. Keep $100 in your carry-on bag and $100 on your person. You never know how difficult it will be to find a bank where you can withdraw money.

- 1 pair of sunglasses

- Snacks

  - Stuff some granola bars and other snacks into your bag before you leave. It is quite possible that you may have a long journey from the airport to where you will be volunteering and might not have access to food that you are quite ready to stomach yet. That granola bar or pack of gummies will help you keep your sanity.

Checked Bag

- Outlet converter and power strip

  - If you are lucky enough to have electricity where you are at, make sure you have the ability to convert it to the currency your American products require. Also, bring a power strip so that you can charge multiple devices at once.

- USB charger

  - Get one with multiple ports that way you can use one outlet to charge your iPod, Kindle, and whatever other devices you have that charge via USB.

- Headlamp

  - This is perhaps the best item you could every buy. I use it every day. Many countries have unreliable power systems and you can often find yourself in black outs. I recommend either Black Diamond or Princeton Tech. Both can be found at REI for a reasonable price.

The Packing List

- Drawstring travel bag

  - Put in a small, drawstring sports bag for day trips. They are compact and prove to be wonderfully useful.

- School supplies

  - Bring a notebook or two, a pack of pens (including red for grading), stickers, rubber bands, and paper clips.

- A few folders/expander files

  - For all of the random papers you will be given. The expander file is especially necessary if you will be teaching and need to process students papers. It's amazing how many there are!

- Nalgene water bottle

  - This is an absolutely necessity. It has allowed me to stay healthy and hydrated throughout my time here.

- Medicine

  - Just in case, bring some essential medicine. This means some Ibuprofen, Dayquil, Nyquil, a pack of Band-Aids, charcoal, and any country specific medications (Malaria, Traveller's Diarrhea, etc.).

- Games

  - I love games and have found that they are a great way to bridge cultural gaps and get to know others at your volunteer location. I brought two packs of cards and Bananagrams. Best decision ever!

- 1 pocket knife

- 1 roll of duct tape or other strong tape

  - I didn't bring this and I regret it. It's just so useful.

- 1 small umbrella

- 1 compact travel towel

  - REI has great ones.

- 1 compact sleeping bag

  - Chances are you will have a bed with sheets where you are volunteering, but you will still need a sleeping bag for when you travel. I recommend both North Face and Marmot sleeping bags. They are durable and have some great lightweight models. A little pricey, but worth it.

- 1 rain jacket/shell

  o Again, my vote is North Face or Marmot. I love their shell jackets. They are compact and do great in the rain.

- 1 thick jacket for traveling to colder regions

- 2 light sweaters

- 1 hoodie

  o I forgot mine, and I miss it so much!

- 5 t-shirts/polos

- 5 dress shirts

  o Only necessary if you need them for teaching. Otherwise, I would just bring 2 for religious services or other formal occasions.

- 2 pairs of athletic shorts

- 2 athletic shirts

- 1 pair of sweat pants

A Gap Year Volunteering

- 1 swimsuit

- 1 pair of pajama pants

- 2 pairs of jeans

- 4 pairs of shorts

- 3 pairs of slacks

  - Again this is more for if you need to dress up regularly. If not, 1 will work.

- 7 pairs of underwear

  - 5 of your regular choice and 2 ExOfficio underwear. I am not joking when I say that this product is absolutely amazing. Their label reads "17 countries, 6 weeks, and one pair of underwear." This might be a bit extreme, but with two pairs, hand washing the one you're not wearing in the evening, you could easily go on a month long trip with just two. They are a bit pricey ($30 each), but are worth every penny.

- 1 dress belt

- 1 regular belt

The Packing List

- 7 pairs of socks

  - 5 regular, 2 dress socks.

- Mesh laundry bag

- 2 pairs of flip flops

  - 1 nice pair (I swear by Rainbow) and 1 cheap pair for showering.

- 1 pair of running/athletic shoes

- 1 pair of regular shoes to go around town in

- 1 pair of dress shoes

- 1 instant shine sponge

  - Alternative to bringing shoe polish and a brush. The sponge is already loaded with polish and you can just scrub a little and your shoe shines right up with no mess. It only costs about $5. Worth it!

- Toiletries

  - Toothbrush

  - Toothpaste

  - Deodorant

  - Face wash

A Gap Year Volunteering

- ○ Retainer

- ○ Nail clippers

- ○ Cologne

- ○ Hair gel

- ○ Chapstick

- ○ Sunscreen

- ○ Insect Repellant

- ○ Shampoo

- ○ Body wash

- ○ Razor

- ○ Shaving cream

- ○ Hand sanitizer

The Flight

So, you've done it. You've packed all of your bags, said your goodbyes, and now find yourself listening to the flight attendants cheerily explain how to use your seat as a flotation device if you crash into the ocean—always a good time. However, in the midst of this, you may find your thoughts wandering. I know that when I was taking off, I started to think about what exactly I had gotten myself into. I mean, once you arrive at this point, there really is no turning back. As soon as the wheels leave the tarmac, it's a done deal. This thought is most likely frightening, but even more likely it is mostly just exciting. You succeeded and are embarking on the experience of a lifetime. I strongly urge you to take a second during that 10+ hour flight to take out your journal and commit a few of these thoughts to paper. Later, you will appreciate it and laugh both at what you were worried about and how you expected everything to be. Also, writing down your goals for the upcoming months will not only help solidify them, but also hold you accountable to achieving them.

Below are some questions that I answered and found helpful:

- Why did I come?

- What kind of a person do I want to be?

    Remember, this is a completely new start. No one knows you, your reputation, your history, your struggles, or your triumphs. You have a unique opportunity to be that person that you have always wanted to be. Put some thought into this question.

- What things would I like to change?

    Maybe in the past you were heavy into the party scene and you want to take a break from it. Perhaps you have struggled with gossiping about others and no longer want to be guilty of it. Or maybe you have been renowned for promiscuity and wish to leave that reputation behind. Maybe you were just a mean person. Whatever your struggles are, this is the perfect chance to overcome them. No one will expect this behavior from you. Your only obstacle will be yourself.

In his book, *What to Say When You Talk to Yourself*, one of my favorite authors, Dr. Helmstetter, says the following:

> "You will become what you think about most; your success or failure in anything, large or small, will depend on your programming—what you accept from others, and what you say when you talk to yourself."[1]

I have found this quote to be completely true. It really is up to you and your thoughts/focus to become the person you want to be. In the book mentioned above, Dr. Helmstetter gives practical advice on how to make changes you want to see in yourself a reality. Definitely a good book to download on that Kindle for the flight over.

- What do I want to get out of this experience?

> Although similar to the past question, this one is much more externally focused. Do you want to

learn a new language? Get better at talking to strangers? Learn how to cook better? Get in shape? Whatever it is, set some goals for yourself and write them down. Doing so makes them a reality more often than not.

- What relationships do I want to keep up and which ones do I need a break from?

    This is in reference to my advice earlier about the benefits of being intentional about your communication and relationships. I urge you to commit to paper any concerns or worries you have regarding specific friendships or relationships. You will find that as you go through the volunteer experience, your perspective will change and you will appreciate seeing how you used to look at something. It´s amazing how just a few months of volunteering can completely alter your perspective.

Once these questions have been answered, sit back, enjoy those in-flight movies, and get ready for the time of your life.

Touchdown

You have started your descent and can see the lights of your future city—it's go time! At this point, the beginning of your experience in a brand new country is fast approaching and you will quickly be confronted with many new and unfamiliar processes, sights, and people. If you keep a few of the following things in mind, you will increase the chances of starting your gap year off right.

The Language Gap

The very best thing that you could do is break out a 3x5 card with some simple phrases and expressions written in the native language. Below are the phrases that I wrote down and found to be extremely helpful.

- Where is my luggage?

- Where can I get a taxi?

- Please.

- Thank you.

- Yes.

- No.

- Nice to meet you.

- What is your name?

- My name is _____."

- I am hungry.

- Where is the bathroom?

- How much does it cost?

While it would be ideal for you to already know the language, a 3x5 card with these things written down will make your entire experience upon arrival that much easier. It is super handy. Promise.

It's Okay to

<u>Feel Overwhelmed</u>

The easiest way that I can get this point across is to provide a brief anecdote of my arrival.

I was absolutely ecstatic to finally start my volunteer experience. I was feeling surprisingly energetic after a 10-hour flight. It may have had something to do with the two venti white mochas I had consumed, but who knows? All that I knew was that the time was finally here! I rushed off the plane ready to tackle the always cumbersome customs process. To my surprise the line was short and entrance into Ecuador was surprisingly easy. They hardly waited to hear why I was in the country. A little disappointed at the ease of it, I headed on to my next "challenge", retrieving my checked luggage. Again, I was met with a painless process. As I walked over to the luggage belt, my two bags were some of the first ones to come sliding down. I would later discover one of these bags no longer contained my MacBook, but for the time being all was well, and I was absolutely stoked on life. I rounded the corner and entered into the main lobby, and then it happened.

I was quite literally swarmed by a horde of what seemed to be miniature Ecuadorians all yelling at me in Spanish. All I could make out was, "Taxi! Hotel! Cheap!" To make matters worse, I didn't see anyone holding a sign with a name anywhere close to "Birkenstock." I, along with my crowd of enthusiastic Ecuadorians, circled the room twice searching everywhere for someone holding a sign with my name on it, but to no avail. I felt absolutely overwhelmed. Here I was, a

A Gap Year Volunteering

6' 4" gringo, clumsily holding onto three bags, with fifteen people half my size yelling at me in a language I didn't understand and with no idea of where or with whom I was going. I had to physically make myself stop for a moment and get it together. I decided that I might as well just go to a hotel in one of the taxis, find some Wi-Fi, and message the school where I was. However, thank goodness, right as I started asking how much a taxi would cost, I spied a small man in the very back corner with the sign "Birnensak." I don't think I have ever been so excited to see my name misspelled. Before I knew it, I was in a car surrounded by my luggage and far too many people, headed to Quito. And so the adventure began.

As you can tell, from the very beginning, your volunteer experience can and most likely will prove to be an adventure. Just embrace it! You are going to be an awkward foreigner who doesn't speak the language and looks different from everyone else. Worst comes to worst, you throw a Hail Mary, get into a taxi and tell them to take you to the American embassy. Now, I never did this, nor did I get anywhere close to it, but it is always there as a last resort. However, I highly suggest taking the alternative route and becoming absolutely shameless about asking for help.

In my experience, if you smile a lot, pull the "I'm a stupid American and am completely lost" card, most people are super friendly and want to help you, relishing in the opportunity to practice their English or at the very least laugh at your feeble attempts to speak their native language. It really is a good time for everyone involved. At their core, I fully believe that most people are naturally good-natured and will do their best to help you. Now this doesn't mean that you should be stupid and jump into a stranger's car or pull out your wallet and start flashing around wads of American dollars. Use common sense, be careful, stay positive and accept the overwhelming moments for what they are—part of the adventure!

Final Journey to
<u>Your Volunteer Site</u>

This will vary from person to person. You may be volunteering a few miles away from the airport or a day's bus journey away from it. Regardless, it can be a long process. It is during this journey that you will find those snacks you stuffed into your luggage at the last minute to be an absolute godsend. In my case, due to mechanical difficulties, I actually found myself stranded for three days in an apartment with a rather silent man who I swear didn't eat. I survived on granola bars and gummy bears.

Another quick note regarding that final journey is that driving in third world countries is an experience like none other. You will quickly see that lanes are nonexistent, everyone honks all the time just for the fun of it, and contact with other cars is a regular occurrence. During my delayed journey I found myself literally thrown onto the dashboard when a bus rear-ended us from behind. Neither of the drivers even batted an eye. Meanwhile, I'm thinking, "What in the world?!?! We were just REAR-ENDED! Are we not stopping to deal with this?...guess not." Immediately following this, I found myself in a car hurtling along mountain roads at 80 km per hour, passing semi-trucks on blind corners. At one point we cut it so close that our side mirror actually scraped the side of a semi. I ended up pulling out my kindle, saying a last minute prayer, and just zoning it all out. What other choice did I have? So, in conclusion, just know that you should not expect American style driving and that it may very well be a rather nerve wracking experience. Know this, expect it, and resign yourself to it. There really is no other alternative.

Arrival & First
Impressions

Congratulations! You have survived the drive to your final destination. At this point you are most likely tired and hungry, your bags seem to weigh more, and you are probably not looking your best. The last thing you are feeling up to is meeting a whole bunch of new people with names that you cannot pronounce who are telling you things you cannot understand... well, this is exactly what's about to happen. Don't worry about how you look or that you are most likely completely illiterate in their language, just break out that smile and get it done. Remember, this is an adventure! You are not always going to be at your best.

Shock Factor

It is quite possible, or rather very likely, that the organization and in specific your accommodations will be somewhat different than what you're used to or even expected. I won't say that organizations are dishonest in regards to their facilities, but I will say that they often leave out quite a bit. Laundry facilities may be a washing machine in a field. A pool may be a dried up hole in the ground. Don't worry about it. This is all part of it and often times these things will change and improve during your time there. In many countries the season determines accessibility to lots of things such as excess water, deliveries of large appliances, etc. Do your best to not make any judgments within the first twenty-four hours of arriving. Just take it all in, stay positive, and laugh at those things that shock you.

Go With the Flow

Often times people are extremely excited to meet the new volunteer regardless of how tired you are or how long you have been traveling. When I arrived, I barely had time to put my stuff in my shockingly exposed room before I was whisked away on yet another bus with three locals who wanted to show me the metropolis that is Santo Domingo, Ecuador. I was tired, and the very last thing I felt like doing was braving the Ecuador traffic again, but what could I do? I came for an adventure and this was it! Just remember to go with the flow. You are making first impressions during this time and the very best thing you can do is show that you are excited to learn about their country, their culture, and that you are honestly overjoyed at the prospect of meeting everyone. You can always catch up on sleep later!

Be Shameless

Butcher the heck out of that language. Everyone will appreciate that you are trying and you will most likely all end up laughing at your linguistic failures. There's no faster way to make friends than laughing at your very first attempt to introduce yourself. By attempting this, you are showing that you value them and their culture and that you genuinely want to get to know them. You will be amazed at how friendly everyone will be.

Journal and Photos

Take as many photos as you can when you arrive, despite your bedraggled appearance. People love nothing more than to take photos in remote countries and you will love to look back at these and reminisce about the beginnings of great friendships.

Also, once you do finally get a moment to yourself, do your best to jot down a few of the many funny memories you have already made. These will most likely include funny language gaffs, names of new friends, and a few first impressions. These will be absolute gold to you in the future!

Living Overseas

You are no longer in America and as such there are a few things that you should remember.

American System

Throw it right out the window. You are now in a new culture with new expectations. Chances are punctuality, definition of cleanliness, forms of greeting, and eye contact are all completely different from what you're used to. This will be off-putting and at times even troublesome, but persevere! You are in a different place and have to adapt.

Frustration

Inevitably, you will have a moment where you feel overwhelmed. Whether you are frustrated with not being able to communicate properly with anyone or are unable to locate basic amenities (laundry, hot shower, etc.) or even are unable to stomach the food…the moment will come. When it does, stop and just take some time for yourself. Whether this means going for a run or simply sitting in your room with your lights off and relaxing—it is okay to freak out a bit and then get it together. To combat moments such as these, I highly suggest developing an "America Fix."

"America Fix"

What is an America Fix? It is exactly what it sounds like. Find some item or activity that reminds you of home and civilization and utilize it when needed. In my case, there is a KFC about a half an hour bus ride away. While I am not particularly fond of this fast food restaurant back in the States, nor do I enjoy paying double what I would in the US, it is nice to have a meal that is familiar. French fries, a chicken sandwich, and a coke. Not particularly healthy, nor is it particularly delicious, but it is familiar and when I sit at that food court in the miniscule Santo Domingo mall, it is as though I am back in the US surrounded by familiar things. It's a wonderful feeling.

Values

A disparity in values may not be apparent at first, probably because you won't understand what people are saying, but eventually it comes to the surface. In America, we are notoriously liberal and lax. This may be in keeping with the country that you are in, but most likely it won't. This can have a variety of ramifications. Just look at my experience for example. I definitely eat meat, love coffee, and am a die-hard Californian who can tackle any obstacle in flip-flops and shorts. At one point or another during my volunteer experience, just about every one of these things has been met with disapproval and honestly I think that that is A-Okay. Some things I have changed and some things I haven't.

First off, I switched from coffee to tea, a substance met with school approval. While this had more to do with the lack of good coffee in central Ecuador, administrators appreciated it nonetheless. Secondly, I quickly found out that while the school was strictly vegetarian, just about everyone ate meat when they went into town or even simply went across the street to a church member's restaurant. So, when I am on campus I'm a vegetarian, and when I'm not feeling that I, along with other faculty members, head across the street and enjoy some "pollo and papas fritas." Next up is my wardrobe challenge. This, I simply haven't changed. While some teachers haven't liked it, when I pointed out that I emailed them ahead of time and asked about dress code and received no information about it, all objections quickly fell by the wayside. I work best when I am comfortable and so I put my foot down on this issue. I already stand out as a pale skinned giant here, what difference does make if I am wearing flip flops and shorts...I can now say after five months...absolutely none!

So, what is my point? Just that you should pay attention to what you are doing and how it coincides with the culture around you. Make an effort to change those things that cause consternation, but stick to your guns when it's important. After all, you're not being paid. Haha!

The Foreigner Card

This feeds off of what I was saying above. While not knowing the language and sticking out like a sore thumb is often frustrating, it can also be a huge advantage to you. First off, you can say and get away with things that others can't. If something clearly needs to be said, but others are unwilling to do so because of cultural limitations, you can live up to your American roots and say it. They may not love it, but many will appreciate it, and in the end everyone will give you a free pass because you are an ignorant American.

Secondly, your lack of fluency may prove to be amazingly useful in numerous situations. Say you accidentally break some obscure cultural rule, all you have to say is that you don't understand what they're saying and that you're sorry. Perhaps one of my most commonly used phrases the first month I was here was, "No entiendo, lo siento." Say you want to stray a bit from rigid classroom structure or maybe you want to skip an unnecessary meeting..."¡No entiendo, lo siento!" Just go for it. Granted, I am not saying to be disrespectful or to grossly abuse this, but just know that it's there when needed. Your ignorance is an asset...at least for a window of time.

Finally, just know that a lot of times you will be a bit of a novelty in the community, which means that individuals generally will have much more patience with you. Enjoy this. You are working hard and if you get a bit of extra leeway or even some home cooked meals out of your foreigner status, all the better. It will help make up for the many hours of initial frustration when you have no idea what is going on.

Be Friendly

Your reputation is very important and how approachable you are is a large part of that. This is made even more difficult if you are not fluent in the native language. To make up for this, you have got to be exceedingly friendly. I'm talking smile on the face 24/7, saying "hi" to strangers as you pass them, and helping out when you see an opportunity. This will go a long way and quickly integrate you into the community.

Don't Say "No"

What do you say when someone shoves a disgusting looking delicacy in front of you? You say, "Thank you" and take a bite. What do you say when someone asks if you want to hike to a lake with crocodiles? You say, "Let me get some mosquito repellant and I'm there." It's that simple. When other volunteers, community members, or even children invite you to something or ask you to do something, 99% of the time your answer should be yes. My first week here in Ecuador, I found myself in the choir that was performing for the 45th anniversary of the school. At that point in time, I didn't speak Spanish and have never really been much of a singer, but hey, I gave it my all and I made a lot of great memories and friends in the process. Just say "yes" when opportunities arise. You won't regret it.

Play Sports

Whether or not you are athletic, this is a must. There is no faster way to get to know an entire community than to take part in their favorite sport. Here in Ecuador there are two sports that are HUGE—futbol (soccer) and Ecua-volley. While I am a 6'4", gangly gringo, I said "what the heck" and jumped in there and I made a lot of good friends in the process, not to mention learned a new favorite game. Ecua-volley is pretty much volleyball with a higher net and they use a soccer ball. I LOVE it!

So, regardless of your athletic abilities or even interest in them, at least give them a shot at the beginning. Everyone will appreciate that you are willing to get out of your comfort zone and that you are trying to get involved in an activity that is culturally valued. Those embarrassing falls, coordination-lacking moments, and downright painful collisions will be well worth it. Trust me!

Travel, Travel, Travel!

This should go without saying. You are in a new country where there are amazing new vistas and experiences around every corner. Take advantage of it and travel as often as fiscally possible! A word of caution though, don't travel alone and if possible, get a local to go with you. It is amazing how much cheaper everything becomes when you have a local flagging down taxis, speaking with hotel concierges, etc. You can automatically assume that if you, an American, ask how much something is, the real price is about half that. To this day, if I stop a taxi and ask them how much it will cost to take me back to school, they immediately say $10. If I have an Ecuadorian with me, it's $5. Every time!

Also, a few more reminders about safety. Please, please keep your wits about you when you go out. You, an American, are a pickpockets dream and like it or not are a target. This means that if possible, you should not break out your wallet or expensive camera in public places. This also means that as often as possible you should only carry small amounts of cash and no debit card on your person. It is not uncommon for particularly brave pickpockets to pull a knife on tourists and get them to withdraw money from the closest ATM. If you don't have your debit card on you, that is automatically not an option. If you are indeed unlucky enough to have an experience with a pickpocket, always, always give them whatever they ask for. This is not the time for bravery, nor will it be worth it. So they steal $50 from you. That sucks, but you are OKAY and you will survive. The same cannot be said if you decide to take on an armed individual in a foreign country with who knows how many accomplices nearby. Just don't risk it. Finally, don't go out at night unless you are with locals. The danger factor instantly goes up tenfold.

Remember, the best thing you can do is not keep anything in your pockets, but rather use that drawstring sports bag I suggested you pack. If in a crowded area you can always wear it in front of you or even under a jacket. Generally, pickpockets would much rather do just that "pick your pocket" when you aren't paying attention. They aren't looking for a confrontation.

One last note—when traveling by bus, be especially vigilant. Don't place your bag on the floor beneath your seat because the person behind you can easily pull it out and relieve it of any valuable items such as your wallet or camera. Keep any expensive items in a bag, on your person, and NEVER in the bottom storage of the bus. Anyone can steal your bag from there by claiming that it's theirs and if it's not your stop, you won't even be nearby to prevent it.

Other Volunteers

Remember, you will share some amazing experiences over the next few months with these people...be nice. Do your absolute best to refrain from gossiping, judging, or offending. Be quick to apologize and happy to help when needed. Also, something that you absolutely must do is make sure that you take some time for yourself. Sometimes, you just need a break and that is absolutely okay. In fact, it's natural. You may only have one other volunteer there who shares your language and months with just that one person without a break can be rough. Think of it more as a marathon. It's better to be friends who often take time out to do their own exploring and have individual experiences than it is to be connected at the hip for the first two months and be sick of each other for the remaining six. Just know your limits and don't be afraid to say that you need some time by yourself. They will understand…and if they don't, they have six months to get over it!

Religion

More often than not, religion plays a large role in a culture. Even if you share the same religion, it will inevitably be practiced in a different way. Do your best to respect how they worship and take part as much as you feel comfortable. For me personally, back in the States I go to church a few times a month, but here they have mandatory services about 9 times a week. This is a LOT for me and I don't understand most of what they are saying, but I bite the bullet and make sure to be in attendance as often as possible. I am not going to lie; your Kindle can do wonders for getting through these services, while still maintaining a respectful image.

Also, they will inevitably want you to be a part of the service, whether it is musically, in preparation, or as the main speaker. Just do it. Try and find common elements that you can connect on and present away. If they don't like it, it's okay; you're a foreigner and will enjoy the benefits of that free pass that you inherently possess.

Learn To Go Without

You are not in America and simply cannot expect to have access to the same products and amenities that you are used to. You have got to learn how to go without and be ready to deal with it while maintaining a positive attitude. There really is no trick for this. All I can say is that learning to go without can be a wonderful experience that reveals the many things you have to be grateful for and that you shouldn't take for granted. It can also be useful in revealing those things that you thought were absolutely necessary, but in reality are superfluous. Think of it as a challenge.

For Those of You Teaching

Right now I am teaching three high school level English classes. Fluency in my classes ranges from just about no comprehension to students who will correct my grammar. Thus, it is inherently difficult to not lose the ones who don't speak English without boring those who are fluent. In this section I am going to impart the lessons that I have learned in the classroom so far.

PS—teaching is challenging, but it is a great time! Students are hilarious and the memories of what you were like in school make it that much funnier! If you have the chance, do it!

Control

You have GOT to own the class, and not let it own you. How can you do this? By adhering to the following:

1.   **Take role.** There is nothing to take control of a class like walking in, pulling out a role sheet and reading out names and marking down who is present. You look like you know what you are doing and it gives you a few moments to come up with a game plan.

2.   **Pray.** This is the best way to get the class to be quiet. Granted this is only an option at religious schools.

3.   **Seating chart.** I didn't do this to begin with and I regretted it. If your class is proving to be loud and difficult, I would highly suggest creating a seating chart. It instantaneously solves so many problems.

4.   **Start a "name on the board" system.** What I did was tell my students that if I had to tell them to be quiet I would write their name on the board. If I had to tell them again, I would put a mark by it, and if it happened again...they were headed to inspección (disciplinarian).

5.   **Display a class schedule.** Write on the board what you will be doing in class that day. That way they know that you have a plan.

89

6. **Give incentives.** For example, just say, "You have 20 minutes to write a 100 word story using this week's vocabulary. Once you're done you can leave." Kids LOVE to get out of class even 5 minutes early. Administration generally doesn't love it, but they get over it.

Projects

Assign projects and give students time in class to work on them. This is especially effective if you tap into some common interests that many of them share. Here in Ecuador I had the seniors do a project on potential universities they could attend. Other classes had to plan out a trip around South America. Projects like these are a great way to keep students interested and to change up the pace a bit. It also cuts down on the amount of grading because you just have one final poster or essay to grade.

Discussion Days

This is my absolute favorite thing to do in the classroom because you really get to know the students. Some of my best memories so far have come from these days. I have had students ask hilarious questions about common misconceptions of the United States. I have learned about troubled childhoods and uncertain futures. I have even come to understand how the Ecuadorian futbol playoff system works. It's these conversation days, where randomness is a necessary element, that you learn the most interesting things. Students love it and so will you.

One word of advice on these days—you will inevitably be asked some personal question by one brave student backed by 5 other giggling ones. I have been asked on a weekly basis whether or not I have a girlfriend, drink, am virgin, think Ecuadorian girls are attractive, etc. Don't shy away from these questions. Just laugh at them; answer them if you don't mind the students knowing that information or if not just be straightforward and say you're not going to answer it. Students love realizing that you will treat them as an adult and will take their questions seriously and will also respect it when you don't provide an answer. If you just blush and start to look embarrassed, it's all over...you've lost your control for the day. You can always regain it the next day, but it takes a while.

English Teachers—

<u>Just Get Them to Talk</u>

It doesn't matter about what subject or whether or not you want to talk about it, the point is to get them to practice speaking in English. On one of our

English discussion days I learned that a percentage of my class regularly visits brothels. No problem, I stopped class and we had a candid, impromptu STD chat...in English. Another time, I asked them to tell me what they did during vacation. Many of them spent it in discotecas partying it up—not a problem. They had to talk about the funniest, appropriate story they could remember from those nights out. Remember, this is not your culture and different things are acceptable at different ages.

When it comes down to it, students are awesome! Rather than judging their interests and extracurricular activities, just provide them with necessary information. If you do this, I promise you will have some very interesting and meaningful conversations. When you are taken aback by something they say, just put it in perspective and realize that at the end of the day you are there to get them to speak English. Whether what they are saying shocks you or not is beside the point. If it's in English, take it!

Cheating

Cheating is one of those things that varies greatly in practice and acceptability from country to country. You will be shocked to see how commonly accepted it can be. Students will sincerely not understand why they shouldn't help their friends on a test. You will have to have conversation after conversation explaining not only why they cannot cheat, but defining exactly what cheating is. Also, it is unwise to just give students a flat zero when you see them cheating. The moment you do this, students will give up and literally leave class. They will also likely have their parents come in and complain (You will be amazed at what side administration may take on this point). Again, this is not the United States.

So what can you do? For me, the absolute best thing has been to write out on the board EXACTLY what I will consider cheating. My list generally looks something like this:

- What is cheating?

    o Giving or receiving answers

    o Texting

    o Talking

    o Looking anywhere besides your test

    o Passing papers

    o Leaving the classroom without permission

I not only write this on the board, but I also attach it to the front of their final exams and have them sign it. That way, there is proof for parents and administration that they were completely aware of what was and was not acceptable. Also, instead of giving them a flat zero, every time I see them breaking any of these rules, I take off a point from their quiz or test. Sometimes it's more than 1 point; it depends on how big of an assignment it is.

If you follow this system, you will greatly decrease the prevalence of cheating.

Games

Students LOVE games. On a weekly basis, my classes have a game day where they split up into four or five groups and compete against one another for extra credit points. Below are some of the games that we play and their descriptions.

Bananagrams

This is a really simple game. You just break out that Bananagrams that I suggested you pack and split up the tiles between all the teams. The first team to utilize all of their tiles with correctly spelled English words wins. This helps students to not only work together, but to also think in English quickly. Also, it's just fun.

Question and Answer

This is the Hail Mary game you play when you have run out of material to teach. You split the class up into groups and let them pick their team names.

The kids love this and it also helps you burn class time. Once they've got names, you just start asking them questions, in English, and the first team to raise their hand and say the correct answer gets a point. You can keep your questions limited to class material or you can stray off into pop culture and beyond. It's really up to you. Regardless, the kids love it and it can be pulled out of your hat of teaching tricks at any time.

Simon Says

This is a great game for helping students remember vocabulary and fully comprehend its implications. It is most suited for action vocabulary such as jump, sit, stand, go back, come forward, etc. If you are unfamiliar with this classic game, which I doubt you are, it is very simple. You stand in front of the class and say, "Simon says to _____." This could be any of your action words. At this point all of the students must perform whatever action you stated. Then you repeat the phrase, but with a different action and again the students must do it. Finally, after a few times of this, you tell the students to do something without the key phrase "Simon Says." If students do the action then they are out. They must ONLY do what "Simon says" to do.

Blindfolded and Guided

If you are lucky enough to get a chapter on directions, this is a phenomenal game. Simply set up an obstacle course, or even just go outside, split the class up into teams and have them choose one person from their team. Blindfold each chosen person and then have their team choose another person to provide English directions throughout the obstacle course. The first team whose representatives complete the obstacle course wins.

Trifecta

This is a pretty intensive game and should only be used when you have a decent amount of time and students who understand quite a bit of English. You first have everyone write down two items or phrases (anything that comes to mind—dinosaur pen, English class, MTV, etc.) on two separate small pieces of paper. Then collect them...and of course screen them. There will be your fair share of anatomical appendages and the occasional cuss word. Throw those out and put the rest in a container. Then have the entire class get in a circle. Give each person a consecutive number going around the circle and then explain that the odd numbered people are on a team and the even numbered people are on a team. They MUST stay seated as they are (perfectly alternated). Then get out a timer (watch, iPod, etc.) and set it to 1 minute. Give the first person the pile of small pieces of paper and explain that they must get their team to guess the word or phrase on each piece of paper by describing it. They cannot use any of the words written on the piece of paper. They must get their team to guess as many words or phrases as possible within 1 minute. At the end of 1 minute, they must pass it to the person next to them who will conveniently be on the opposing team...and so you go down the circle with each person having 1 minute of time. You must keep track of how many each team guesses as you go. Once all the papers have been guessed, you put them back in a pile and start the process again. This time however, they have to act it out without any words. Finally, after all of them have been acted out, you start the process all over again, but this time they can only say one word to hint at what it is. This word cannot be on the paper. Additionally, there can be no actions accompanying the word. After this process is complete, the team who correctly guessed the most wins.

Homework

Don't go crazy here. The school where I teach is really not big on homework, so attempting to actually get every student to do homework regularly is an absolute pain because there is not much parental or institutional support. What I have found works best is to assign a small homework assignment two or three times a week and give them the last ten minutes in class to work on it. That way they only have to do a small portion by themselves or possibly none at all. However, if homework is more prevalent at your school, go for it. Just do your best not to make it superfluous...students know what busy work is and they hate it.

Grades

This is when that computer comes in handy. Excel has saved my life and kept both my sanity and enthusiasm intact while here in Ecuador. You will be amazed at how easily papers can get mixed up, foreign names look similar, and all types of mishaps occur. A simple Excel document with their names, the assignments, and their grade will make your life a million times easier...especially when grades are due.

Important

Classroom Phrases

These are a few phrases you should know how to say in the native language.

- Sit down please.

- Please be quiet.

- Listen.

- Raise your hand.

- Leave the classroom.

- No cheating.

- No talking.

- Get out a piece of paper.

- No throwing.

- No spitting.

- No hitting.

- No screaming.

- Put that down.

- Stop

- You have homework.

- Pen

- Pencil

- Sentences

- Words

- #1-10

- Correct

- Incorrect

A Gap Year Volunteering

- Yes

- No

- Homework

- Quiz

- Test

- Do you understand?

Final Thoughts

It is absolutely impossible to fully describe what a year serving as a volunteer does for both the people you are serving and your own self-development. I firmly believe that everyone should take some time out and spend a year abroad, if possible. My advice to you, the future volunteer, is to commit to the decision, embrace the adventure, and just live every second of it to the fullest! Never again in your life will you have such a unique opportunity to discover another culture, new things about yourself, and put past struggles or concerns behind you. It really is one of the best decisions you could ever make. Don't doubt it and don't delay it! GO! GO! GO!

"I learned that courage was not the absence of fear, but the triumph over it. I felt fear myself more times than I can remember, but I hid it behind a mask of boldness. The brave man is not he who does not feel afraid, but he who conquers that fear."[2]

-Nelson Mandela
Long Walk To Freedom

Special Thanks

I would like to thank my fellow volunteers as well as the rest of my Ecuadorian family here at Colegio Adventista del Ecuador. It has been the experience of a lifetime. A huge thank you to my friends and family back in the States who made my volunteer year possible and continue to enrich my life in so many ways. Also, a special thanks to Jeanne Vories and the Walla Walla University Student Missions Department. Your tireless work each year enables dozens of volunteers to change the lives of countless people around the world. Finally, and most importantly, I thank God for his wisdom and guidance throughout this entire process.

Appendix A

Adventist Church Missions

Hesaidgo.net

Global Vision International

Gviausa.com

Peace Corps

Peacecorps.gov

United Planet

Unitedplanet.org

Appendix B

Bookingbuddy.com

Great way to search multiple websites for cheap tickets without having to re-enter in airports and dates for each one.

Kayak.com

Kayak has a great tool that allows you to set up the flight you are looking for and then they email you when it changes its price drastically. It also predicts whether prices will rise or fall in the future.

Onetravel.com

I have bought nearly every international plane ticket through this website. It is consistently the cheapest and I have never had a problem with my flights.

Notes

1. Helmstetter, Shad. *What to Say When You Talk to Your Self*. New York: Pocket, 1992. Print.

2. Mandela, Nelson. *Long Walk to Freedom*. Boston New York London: Back Bay Little, Brown and, 1995. Print.